New Baby Therapy

New Baby Therapy

written by
Lisa O. Engelhardt

illustrated by
R.W. Alley

ONE
CARING
PLACE

Abbey Press

Text © 1997 by Lisa O. Engelhardt
Illustrations © 1997 by St. Meinrad Archabbey
Published by One Caring Place
Abbey Press
St. Meinrad, Indiana 47577

Library of Congress Catalog Number
97-77583

ISBN 0-87029-307-9

Printed in the United States of America

Foreword

Congratulations on your new little bundle of blessing! No one could have prepared you for the wonder and joy you feel at this miracle of life and love. Neither could anyone prepare you for the fatigue and disruption and worry! Like many new parents, you might agree that this is "the best of times and the worst of times."

Change is the order of the day: not just the diapers, of course, but your entire life. Your roles and responsibilities and priorities are changing—as are your schedule and your relationship with each other. Your baby is changing rapidly, too, growing and developing almost right before your eyes. Soon you will wonder where this precious newborn time went.

New Baby Therapy helps you to make the most—and cope with the worst—of this special time. Written by a mother of three, this little volume empathizes with the bewildering experience of having a new baby in the house, while offering tips for nurturing your infant and yourselves. May it help you to find the patience to endure, the peace to enjoy this baby who won't be a baby for long!

1.

A new baby is a miracle
of love and life.
Congratulations on
this blessed event!

2.

God called <u>you</u> to be parents to this special baby, because no other parents can do the job better. Have faith in God and yourselves.

3.

The moment you hold your new baby, you will know that any pain or anxiety that preceded your baby's arrival was worth it. Enjoy!

4.

Savor the smells and sounds and feel of your baby: the powder-fresh sweetness, the gurgles and coos, the velvety softness of her skin. Take time just to be with your baby—to hold her, to love her.

5.

Sing to your baby, rock her, dance with her, talk to her, answer her babble. She will thrive in body, mind, and spirit, and know from her earliest days how much she is loved and cherished.

6.

A new baby is utterly dependent on you—for nourishment, care, and affection. You may be amazed at the strong protectiveness and deep tenderness this brings out in you. Let your natural, God-given instincts help you to lovingly nurture your child.

7.

At the same time, a newborn's fragileness and helplessness can make the responsibility of caring for him somewhat scary. Trust that God will give you what you need, when you need it, to nurture this little life entrusted to you.

8.

Some parents do not experience instant maternal or paternal instinct. Don't add to your stress by worrying needlessly or judging yourself. With time and practice, you'll feel like "a natural."

9.

Your baby's arrival has been preceded by months of preparation and anticipation. You may feel overjoyed or overwhelmed, ecstatic or exhausted. All of these feelings are natural. Share your feelings and needs with your spouse.

10.

Even if you carried this baby in your womb for nine months, he is still a newcomer to your family, a stranger that you need to get acquainted with. Give yourself time to get to know him, his temperament and schedule, his likes and dislikes.

11.

Right from the start, your baby will have his own unique personality, different from any other child. Treat him as the individual that he is, giving him the special care and love he requires. Delight in his uniqueness.

12.

Give yourself permission to
let the dishes pile up, let the
dust bunnies multiply, let the
housework go. Put your regular
life on hold—so you have time
to hold your baby.

13.

Taking care of this new little person can be exhausting. You may be sore from delivery, tired from not enough sleep, worn out from all the excitement. Sleep when the baby sleeps. Snatch a nap whenever you can.

14.

The best way to guarantee
a happy, healthy baby is to
nurture yourselves as happy,
healthy parents. Try to get your
minimum daily requirement of
nutritious food, sleep (as much
as possible), exercise, prayer,
hugs, relaxation, and fun.

15.

Though you may not believe it when you're feeling tired and cranky, someday you'll wish you had this newborn time back again. Seize the day! Hug your baby!

16.

Your family is undergoing rapid change right now. The changes in your baby, from day to day, are dramatic. You are changing and growing too—in your new identities as the parents of this baby. Change can be stressful. Be patient and tolerant as you adjust.

17.

Baby-tending can be a full-time job—for Mom <u>and</u> Dad. Take as much leave from work as possible, so that you can share the blessings and the burdens of this time. Be a team twenty-four hours a day, and be sure to remember the three most caring words you can say in the middle of the night: "I'll get up."

18.

If you have another child, try to spend one-on-one time with her each day. Let her know how special she is and always will be to you, how no one could ever take her place. Let her help with the baby, and then be sure to praise her efforts.

19.

If friends and relatives want to come and see the new baby, let them know when would be a good time. Don't worry about cleaning up, fixing yourself up, or entertaining your visitors. Your baby is the star.

20.

If a constant stream of visitors starts to make you feel smothered, know when to say no. Politely postpone visits and "hide out" for a day: close the blinds, turn on the answering machine, treat yourself to your favorite soothing activity.

21.

Welcome help from those who offer—to bring a casserole for dinner, to hold the baby while you shower or nap, to dust and vacuum. Everyone rejoices with you in your good fortune—and wants to help you handle it! It takes a village to raise a baby.

22.

It can be a shock to discover how long it takes to get ready to go out, all the equipment you need, how hard it can be to work around a baby's schedule. Plan ahead, expect delays, and loosen up. With new babies, the best-laid plans often go astray.

23.

Everyone loves babies. Enjoy the attention from friends and relatives, the smiles and comments from folks everywhere you go. Pass the love around!

24.

People may offer you unsolicited advice on how to care for your baby. Know that this advice is offered with the best of intentions, but that you have the right to do what you judge best for your baby and you.

25.

Babies go through stages of development in what will seem to you later as lightning speed. If your baby is cranky, colicky, teething, or waking up several times a night, remember: This too shall pass. Ask your pediatrician about any persistent problems.

26.

With all the time- and energy-consuming duties of parenthood, it's easy to neglect your relationship as a couple. Take time for just the two of you. Schedule a date—alone. Friends and relatives make wonderful and willing babysitters. Take a leap of faith and leave.

27.

Get together with other parents to swap baby stories, to vent and lament, to share problems and progress. It's healthy and helpful to get encouragement and advice from those who have "been there"—and to pass along your own wisdom.

28.

New moms sometimes feel discouraged with their physical appearance—especially if they don't immediately shrink down to pre-pregnancy size. Try to stick to a nutrition and exercise plan, and reward yourself for every pound lost or muscle toned.

29.

Many new parents experience fluctuating moods in the weeks after the arrival of the baby. If caring for your baby seems completely overwhelming, however, or you continue to feel depressed or extremely emotional, be sure to let your physician know.

30.

If you return to work after maternity or paternity leave, you may feel that nobody can care for your child as well as you, and that you are leaving part of yourself behind when you walk out the door. Expect to feel distressed for awhile, but know that it does get better.

31.

Your baby will accomplish many firsts in the months to come: first smile, first tooth, rolling over, crawling, standing up, and that big first step. Take pleasure in these firsts, and let your little one know how proud you are.

32.

Preserve your memories of this precious time—through photos, videos, tape recordings, notes, a baby album. Joy remembered lasts forever.

33.

It's amazing how quickly babies outgrow their clothes, how soon they don't fit lengthwise on your lap anymore. Though it can be sad to see your baby get bigger, be glad for his progress—it's a testament to your good care—and know he will never outgrow your love.

34.

A new baby calls former priorities into question, as you gain a new sense of the meaning and mission of your life. Take time, make time, for what really matters.

35.

Parents raise children, but children raise parents, too. A new baby will teach you depths of tenderness, patience, and selflessness you would never have thought possible. Let yourself learn and grow.

36.

Your baby will inspire in you deep care and compassion for all children everywhere. Forever after, when a child cries or is in need, you will want to respond. Let parenthood expand your heart.

LOST
PARENTS
BOOTH

ROLLER
COASTER

37.

You never know how much love you can feel until you have a new baby. This child will grip your finger and your heart with incredible force—and your life will never be the same. Thank God every day for the gift of your new baby.

38.

May you have the patience to endure, the peace to enjoy this baby who won't be a baby for long. God bless you and your new little one!

Lisa O. Engelhardt serves as editorial director of the Product Development division of Abbey Press. The author of several Elf-help books, she lives with her husband and three children in Lawrenceburg, Indiana.

Illustrator for the Abbey Press Elf-help Books, **R.W. Alley** also illustrates and writes children's books. He lives in Barrington, Rhode Island, with his wife, daughter, and son.

The Story of the Abbey Press Elves

The engaging figures that populate the Abbey Press "elf-help" line of publications and products first appeared in 1987 on the pages of a small self-help book called *Be-good-to-yourself Therapy*. Shaped by the publishing staff's vision and defined in R.W. Alley's inventive illustrations, they lived out author Cherry Hartman's gentle, self-nurturing advice with charm, poignancy, and humor.

Reader response was so enthusiastic that more Elf-help Books were soon under way, a still-growing series that has inspired a line of related gift products.

The especially endearing character featured in the early books—sporting a cap with a mood-changing candle in its peak—has since been joined by a spirited female elf with flowers in her hair.

These two exuberant, sensitive, resourceful, kindhearted, lovable sprites, along with their lively elfin community, reveal what's truly important as they offer messages of joy and wonder, playfulness and co-creation, wholeness and serenity, the miracle of life and the mystery of God's love.

With wisdom and whimsy, these little creatures with long noses demonstrate the elf-help way to a rich and fulfilling life.

Elf-help Books

...adding "a little character" and a lot
of help to self-help reading!

Garden Therapy
#20116 $4.95   ISBN 0-87029-325-7

Elf-help for Busy Moms
#20117 $4.95   ISBN 0-87029-324-9

Trust-in-God Therapy
#20119 $4.95   ISBN 0-87029-322-2

Elf-help for Overcoming Depression
#20134 $4.95   ISBN 0-87029-315-X

New Baby Therapy
#20140 $4.95   ISBN 0-87029-307-9

Grief Therapy for Men
#20141 $4.95   ISBN 0-87029-306-0

Living From Your Soul
#20146 $4.95   ISBN 0-87029-303-6

Teacher Therapy
#20145 $4.95   ISBN 0-87029-302-8

Be-good-to-your-family Therapy
#20154 $4.95   ISBN 0-87029-300-1

Stress Therapy
#20153 $4.95   ISBN 0-87029-301-X

Making-sense-out-of-suffering Therapy
#20156 $4.95   ISBN 0-87029-296-X

Get Well Therapy
#20157 $4.95   ISBN 0-87029-297-8

Anger Therapy
#20127 $4.95   ISBN 0-87029-292-7

Caregiver Therapy
#20164 $4.95   ISBN 0-87029-285-4

Self-esteem Therapy
#20165 $4.95   ISBN 0-87029-280-3

Take-charge-of-your-life Therapy
#20168 $4.95   ISBN 0-87029-271-4

Work Therapy
#20166 $4.95   ISBN 0-87029-276-5

Everyday-courage Therapy
#20167 $4.95   ISBN 0-87029-274-9

Peace Therapy
#20176 $4.95   ISBN 0-87029-273-0

Friendship Therapy
#20174 $4.95   ISBN 0-87029-270-6

Christmas Therapy (color edition)
#20175 $5.95   ISBN 0-87029-268-4

Grief Therapy
#20178 $4.95   ISBN 0-87029-267-6

More Be-good-to-yourself Therapy
#20180 $3.95   ISBN 0-87029-262-5

Happy Birthday Therapy
#20181 $4.95   ISBN 0-87029-260-9

Forgiveness Therapy
#20184 $4.95   ISBN 0-87029-258-7

Keep-life-simple Therapy
#20185 $4.95   ISBN 0-87029-257-9

Be-good-to-your-body Therapy
#20188 $4.95   ISBN 0-87029-255-2

Celebrate-your-womanhood Therapy
#20189 $4.95   ISBN 0-87029-254-4

Acceptance Therapy (color edition)
#20182 $5.95   ISBN 0-87029-259-5

Acceptance Therapy
#20190 $4.95   ISBN 0-87029-245-5

Keeping-up-your-spirits Therapy
#20195 $4.95   ISBN 0-87029-242-0

Play Therapy
#20200 $4.95   ISBN 0-87029-233-1

Slow-down Therapy
#20203 $4.95   ISBN 0-87029-229-3

One-day-at-a-time Therapy
#20204 $4.95   ISBN 0-87029-228-5

Prayer Therapy
#20206 $4.95   ISBN 0-87029-225-0

Be-good-to-your-marriage Therapy
#20205 $4.95   ISBN 0-87029-224-2

Be-good-to-yourself Therapy (hardcover)
#20196 $10.95   ISBN 0-87029-243-9

Be-good-to-yourself Therapy
#20255 $4.95   ISBN 0-87029-209-9

Available at your favorite giftshop or bookstore—
or directly from One Caring Place, Abbey Press
Publications, St. Meinrad, IN 47577.
Or call 1-800-325-2511.